EASYWAY GUIDES

GUIDE
TO PLANNING A WEDDING

Anna Bennett

Easyway Guides

Easyway Guides
Brighton BN2 4EG

© Straightforward Publishing 2006

ISBN 1900694 83 2

Printed by Webspeedbooks Bedfordshire
www.webspeedbooks.com

Cover design by Straightforward Graphics

Contents

1 Marriage and cohabitation 15

Marriage	15
Marriages must be voluntary	16
Marriages which can be annulled	17
Grounds for annulment	17
Getting engaged to be married	18
Marriage formalities	19
Religious ceremonies	19
Church of England	19
Publishing Banns	20
Common licence	21
Special licence	21
Superintendent registrars certificate	21
Divorced persons and Church of England	22
Other denominations	23
Civil ceremonies	23
Witnesses	24
Marriages abroad	24
Effects of marriage	25
Surnames	26
Joint assets	26
Common parenthood	26
Marital confidences	27
Marriages of convenience	27
Cohabitation	28
Taxation	29
Cohabitees as husband and wife	29
Agreements	30

2 The Engagement   33

Engagement party   33
Organization of the wedding   34
The responsibilities of the groom   36
The role of the father of the bride   36
The role of the bridesmaid   36
The role of the best man   37
The role of the ushers   38
Toastmaster   38
Paying for the wedding   38
Groom   38
Bride   39
The father of the bride   39
Invitations to the wedding   40
Formal weddings   41
Preparing the guest list   42
Sample guest list   43
Alternative invitations   44
The reception   44
Table seating plan   45
Wedding speeches   46
Cutting the cake   50
Display of gifts   50

3 Main decisions prior to a wedding   51

Setting the date   51
Church weddings   52
Civil ceremonies   53
Marrying outside the United Kingdom   54
Planning the wedding reception   55
Choosing the menu   57
Accommodation   57

Attendants   57
What to wear   58
Bridal dress   58
Hiring a dress   58
Made-to-measure   59
Bridesmaids and Matron-of-Honour   59
Dress for the men   60
Transport   61
Transport before the ceremony   61
After the ceremony   62
After the reception   62
Organising photography and videos   63
Arranging flowers   64
The wedding cake   65
The wedding stationary   66
Fees for marriage   67
Wedding insurance   68
Getting your wedding arranged   69
Wedding gifts   69
The honeymoon   76

4 Different types of wedding ceremony   77

Anglican ceremony   77
Buddhist wedding   81
Catholic wedding   82
Christian Scientist   84
Hindu Ceremonies   84
Humanist weddings   85
Jewish weddings   86
Muslim weddings   88
Non-Conformist weddings   88
Pagan ceremonies   89
Quaker weddings   90
Single-sex partnerships   91
Unitarian   91

5 Planning the wedding -budget for the ceremony   93

Church of England wedding   93
Register Office wedding   94

6 Budgeting for the overall wedding   97

Wedding planner   98

Useful addresses
Index

Introduction

Without doubt, getting married must rank as one of the big events in life. This is a day that will never be forgotten, and this book will try to ensure that it will never be forgotten for all the right reasons.

This book covers conventional heterosexual weddings although does recognise the introduction of civil partnerships. Those who have entered into a civil partnership can also utilise the many useful areas of this book, such as planning and budgeting for a wedding.

The first chapter covers general points relating to marriage, such as the law and also other areas such as tax and property. The intention is to provide and overview of the institution of marriage.

The subsequent chapters cover all the elements of a wedding, such as the initial engagement and the planning of the big day, including the main players such as the best man and bridesmaids, not forgetting the bride and groom! The biggest expense of the wedding day is covered, the reception, which always needs careful planning. Also Included are outline budgeting frameworks to ensure that all costs are covered.

Alternative wedding ceremonies (other than traditional Church of England) are also covered, such as Buddhist,

Muslim Pagan, Unitarian, Christian Scientist and Non-Conformist.

Getting married is a big event for all concerned, not least the bride and groom. If it goes well, it will be a day to remember. It may be expensive but it is so important that accurate planning is needed.

Of course, there are those who do not desire a big wedding and this book will also show you how to do it on a shoestring. Whichever way you choose to go this book should help immeasurably in the planning of the big day.

Good luck!

This book is dedicated to Morgana, without whose love and help I would be a very different person.

1

Marriage and Cohabitation

The law of England states that marriage is the 'voluntary union for life of one man and one woman to the exclusion of all others'.

Much has changed in family life over the years and today, marriages break up with alarming frequency and more and more people choose to live together as opposed to marrying.

Before we discuss the preparations for getting married, which is the main aim of this book, we should look at the institution of marriage and how it works within the law. We will look at who can get married, the engagement, marriage formalities, effect's of marriage, cohabitation and agreements.

Marriage

The law states that, in order to marry, a person must:

a) be unmarried
b) be over the age of 18

You are also legally a single person if your previous marriage has been annulled. Basically, anyone who wants to marry must be a single person in the eyes of the law. A person must be over 18. If a person is aged between 16-18 parental consent must be gained. A marriage where one of the persons is under 16 is absolutely void. If someone marries between the ages of 16-18 the marriage is voidable as opposed to void (see below). Parents, guardians or the courts must consent to a marriage for someone between 16-18 years old.

No marriage can take place between close relations, i.e. blood relations, or non-blood relations where the relation is so close that a ban on intermarriage is still imposed. Adopted children are generally treated in law as blood relatives. Brothers-in-law and sisters-in-law can marry as can step parent and stepchild if the stepchild has not been raised as a child of the family and is over 21 years old.

Marriages must be voluntary

A marriage must be voluntary and not brought about through coercion. This brings about a problem in law when arranged marriages take place, as is the custom in certain ethnic groups. In general the law does not interfere with arranged marriages.

However, the courts will get involved if it is felt that there is duress and there is a threat of injury to life or liberty or a child is threatened with expulsion from home or community.

Marriages which can be annulled

Void marriages
Certain marriages are regarded in law as void. This means that, in the eyes of the law the marriage has never taken place at all. Marriages are void where

- one of the parties is under 18
- the parties are closely related
- one of the parties is not a single person, i.e. the marriage is bigamous or polygamous.
- The parties are regarded in law as being of the same sex.

Certain marriages are regarded in law as valid until they are annulled. These are 'voidable' marriages and, in the eyes of the law can be annulled by either party.

Grounds for annulment

In order for a court to annul a voidable marriage the following grounds have to be demonstrated:

a) the marriage has not been consummated

17

b) the husband or wife had not understood the nature of the ceremony
c) the marriage was to someone of unsound mind
d) the marriage was to someone with venereal disease.

Getting engaged to be married

An engagement is not a precondition of marriage, as it once was. This is often the case, however. A couple will, after engagement, publicly announce their intention to be married. Legal disputes can, however, arise and couples can dispute ownership of property and gifts. An engagement ring is regarded as an outright gift in the eyes of the law.

If money has been expended on larger items, such as a house, in the anticipation of marriage, and the marriage has fallen through then this will become a legal dispute with each case turning on its own merit and the circumstances of any contract, written or unwritten. Certain insurance companies can offer insurance against weddings falling through or being cancelled. Cover can also be obtained for honeymoons falling through.

If a couples wedding falls through they are legally obliged to return any wedding gifts received to their senders.

Marriage formalities

For a marriage to be valid, a formal licence and a formal ceremony are necessary. Authority to licence marriages is given to a priest of the Anglican Church and to civil officials (registrars). Every couple, therefore, must obtain permission to marry from an Anglican church or from a civil official. Many couples, because of cost, choose to marry in a registry office.

Religious ceremonies

Religious ceremonies are categorized according to whether they are solemnized by:

- The Anglican Church, including the Church of Wales
- Jews or Quakers (for whom special rules apply under the Marriage Act 1949)
- Some other recognized religion.

We have lived in a diverse ethnic society for many years and the rules governing marriage and religion are largely outmoded and in need of change. This will inevitably happen over time.

Church of England-licence to marry

About half of all religious marriage ceremonies take place

in the Church of England. There are four ways to effect the necessary preliminaries for an Anglican marriage. Only one may be used. In order to obtain consent to marry in the Church of England you must either:

- publish banns

or obtain one of the following:

- a common ecclesiastical licence
- a 'special licence' also from the ecclesiastical authorities
- a superintendent registrars certificate from the civil authorities.

Publishing banns

The banns, or the names of the couple who intend to marry, have to be read aloud (published) in the church of the parish where the couple are resident. If the couple are resident in different parishes then the banns must be read in each parish church, in one or other of which the ceremony will take place. The priest needs seven days notice in writing from both parties before the banns can be read. The priest has to read them audibly in church on three successive Sundays. If there is no objection from any member of the congregation then, after the third reading the marriage can take place. If any objections are raised, and voiced audibly by a member of the congregation then the banns are void.

Common licence

This dispenses with the banns and is given by the Bishop of the diocese. You must make a sworn affidavit that there is no impediment to the marriage and that any necessary parental consent has been given and that you have resided in the parish for 15 days.

Once granted, the licence to marry has immediate effect and is valid for three months. It will specify the church or chapel in which the marriage is to take place.

Special licence

This is issued by the Archbishop of Canterbury and enables a marriage to take place at any time or place. It also dispenses with the 15-day residence period. To get such a licence, which would for example be applicable if one of the parties was seriously ill, a sworn statement is required.

Superintendent registrars certificate

Although it is the norm for a marriage in the Church of England to take place after banns have been read, or after obtaining a licence from church authorities, an Anglican wedding can take place after a superintendent registrars certificate has been obtained. The parties must give notice to a superintendent registrar in the district in which they have resided for at least seven days before giving notice. They must make a solemn declaration that there are no lawful impediments to their union and that they meet the residential requirements. In the case of persons between 16-18, that they have parental consent. If the parties live in different districts then notice must be given in each district.

The notice is displayed in the superintendent's office for 21 days. At the end of that period, provided there are no objections, the certificate is issued. The marriage can take place in a church within the superintendent's district. The consent of the minister of the church must be obtained.

Divorced person wishing to marry in the Church of England

Where either party is a divorced person, a remarriage cannot be solemnized in the Church of England. This does not apply where the marriage has been annulled.

Other stipulations to a Church of England Wedding are laid down in the law, as follows:

- the marriage must be in an unlocked church

- between the hours of 8am and 8pm
- two witnesses must be present

Other denominations and religions

If you belong to another denomination or religion other than the Church of England, you must first obtain permission from the civil authorities to marry. There are four ways of meeting the legal requirements, of which only one need be used:

- a superintendent registrar's certificate
- a superintendent registrar's certificate with a licence. This has a residence requirement of 15 days.

For those seriously ill or detained, special provisions under the Marriage Act 1983 and the Marriage (Registrar General's Licence) Act 1970 will apply.

Weddings for Jews and Quakers can take place anywhere or at any time under the Marriage Act according to their own practices. The marriage is solemnized by a person designated for the purpose.

Civil ceremonies

The General Register Office will issue a form 357, which provides notes on the legal formalities of marrying.

Marriages in a register office require a solemn declaration from both bride and groom according to the civil form:

- that they know of no impediment to their union
- that they can call upon those present as witnesses that they take each other as lawful wedded wife or husband.

The two witnesses present then sign the register.

The superintendent registrar and the registrar must both be present at a civil wedding, which can only take place in a registry office, except in very unusual circumstances where people are ill or otherwise confined.

Witnesses

All marriages, without exception, be they religious or civil, require two witnesses to the ceremony. The witnesses need not know the couple. After a ceremony the witnesses sign the register and a marriage certificate is issued.

Marriages abroad

Generally speaking, a marriage that takes place in another country is recognised as valid in this country. However, all the laws associated with marriage in England and

Wales must apply, such as the age restriction and the single person status. It is essential if a person intends to marry abroad that they seek legal advice in order to ascertain the status of the marriage in the UK.

Effects of a marriage

Being married confers a legal status on husband and wife. In general, questions of status, rights and duties concern the following:

Duty to live together

Husband and wife have a duty to live together. If one spouse leaves the other for good then an irretrievable breakdown has occurred (see next chapter on divorce).

Duty to maintain

Spouses have a duty to maintain one another. This extends to children, obviously, and becomes a particular problem on breakdown of marriage.

Sexual relationship

Husband and wife are expected to have sexual relations. Failure to consummate a marriage, as we have seen, can lead to annulment of a marriage.

Fidelity

Husband and wife are expected to be faithful to one another. Adultery is one of the main grounds for divorce.

Surnames

A wife can take her husband's surname but is not under a legal duty to do so. A wife's right to use the husbands surname will survive death and divorce. A husband can also take a wife's surname although this is unusual. Occasionally, couples will adopt both surnames.

If a wife changes her surname to her husbands she can do so informally, simply by using the name. However, change of surname has to be declared to institutions such as banks and a marriage certificate has to be produced.

Joint assets

The matrimonial home as well as family income become assets of a marriage. As we will see, a breakdown of marriage can lead to long and costly battles over assets of a marriage.

Common parenthood

Husband and wife automatically acquire parental responsibility for the children of their marriage. If the couple separate the courts can alter the relationship between parent and child.

Marital confidences

Secrets and other confidences of married life shared between husband and wife are protected by law. This is particularly relevant in this day and age where the tabloids invade the lives of people as never before. Married, and even divorced, persons can obtain injunctions to stop publication of confidential information.

Marriages of convenience

The laws surrounding such marriages have been gradually tightening up. Such marriages are seen as sham devices to get around UK immigration law. In order to issue a person with an entry clearance certificate to enter the UK as an affianced person or spouse, the immigration authorities will want to be sure that:

a) the 'primary' purpose is to get married and that a separation will not take place after marriage and entry
b) that spouses intend to live together as husband and wife
c) if the couple are not already married that the marriage will take place within six months.

It also has to be shown that parties to the marriage will settle in the UK.

Cohabitation

Despite peoples perceptions to the contrary, there is no such thing as 'common law' relationships, i.e. people living together unmarried, as man and wife. As far as the law is concerned they are two legal individuals. There is no duty to cohabit, no duty to maintain. With regard to children, the duty of care usually falls on the mother. However, in the case of unmarried couples, both mother and father can enter into a parental responsibility agreement which should place them in a similar position to married couples in regards to responsibility to children.

If a couple who cohabit and have children do separate then there is a duty on the father (absent parent) to maintain the child until they reach the age of 17.

Effect on assets

The courts can decide what split will take place in regard to assets of a cohabiting couple. This share is based on concrete facts of the individual's contributions. A live-in partner has no right to occupy the family home under the Matrimonial Homes Act 1973, in the event of breakdown of relationship. However, the law has tightened up in this area.

Taxation

There are important differences between the tax position of married and cohabiting couples. These are as follows:

- cohabiting couples cannot take advantage of the taxation rules between husband and wife that ensure gifts between husband and wife are free of capital gains tax

- they cannot take advantage of the fact that on the death of a spouse, the other spouse inherits free of inheritance tax

However, as these rules change frequently you should refer to your local take office for advice. You should also take advice concerning wills and pensions.

Where the law treats cohabitees as husband and wife

There are certain areas where the law will afford the same protection to cohabitees as married people:

- Victims of domestic violence are entitle to protection whether married or not

- With regard to security of tenure, a couple who live together as husband and wife will be entitled to joint security whether married or not

- Certain social security benefits are available for live in couples. You should seek advice from the local benefits agency

- A duty to maintain the children of a relationship is imposed-irrespective of whether married or not

- Under the Fatal Accidents Act, dependant cohabitees, who have lived together for two years or more may be entitled to damages on his or her death.

Agreements

Cohabitees can enter into agreements to protect property and other assets in the event of splitting up. Married couples also do this.

Contracts between married couples

At common law, a husband 'administered' his wife's property. In effect, a woman no longer owned property after she married. The law moves on thankfully! Today, property that a woman owned before marriage remains her own. If divorce takes place the question to be considered is whether the property has become an asset of the marriage. Each case will turn on its own merit. In view of the courts wide powers to determine what happens to assets after marriage, few couples enter into agreements (pre-nuptial agreement being the most common). However, the wealthier the person, the wiser it is to enter into such an agreement.

Cohabitation agreement

When unmarried couples part, the courts have little powers to determine the split of assets. In relation to cohabitation agreements, there are problems under the law of contract. When parties enter into a contract, both sides have to offer something towards the contract. This is called 'consideration' for the contract. In an agreement to cohabit it would be difficult to define consideration other than on the basis of a sexual relationship. Nevertheless it is wise to have an agreement as a basis, or structure, of the relationship when it concerns assets.

Guide to Planning a Wedding

2

The Engagement

The preliminary step, for a good many people, but not all, to getting married is to inform parents, relatives and friends. After parents have been told of the (hopefully to them) good news it is then time to inform friends and relatives. This is normally done by a card. Following this it is custom to announce an engagement in the local or national papers. This is done by the parents of the bride. The announcement should be worded according to the circumstances.

If the parents of the bride to be are deceased then it is customary for the happy couple to insert an advertisement themselves. The newspaper that the advert is being placed in can advise on the wording as this will differ according to the marriage.

A public announcement of an engagement should never be made if one of the couple is legally married. It is custom to wait until a marriage has legally ended.

Engagement party

If it is intended to have a party to celebrate an engagement, the brides family will usually arrange this.

At some point during the party the father of the bride will make an official announcement, giving a toast and welcoming the groom-to-be to the family.

Organization of the wedding

The bride is very involved in the organization of the wedding and a fair degree of responsibility will fall on the shoulders of bride and mother. The bride and mother will usually organise the following:

- arrange for both sets of parents to meet together if this has not already occurred

- discuss the overall plans for the wedding with the groom and both sets of parents. Although traditionally weddings are paid for by the brides father, it is common for both parties to share the costs where agreed as one person paying for all can be an unacceptable burden

- compile a list of friends and relatives to be informed and arrange the engagement party

- bride and groom-to-be select wedding attendants and inform them of their role

- draw up a list of guests to be invited

- draw up the wedding gift list with the grooms assistance

- draw up a budget for the whole event

- if necessary, arrange wedding insurance

- choose a venue depending on the type of wedding chosen

- visit the registrar or minister depending on what is chosen, church or registry office, deal with the legal requirements

- book the photographer, transport, entertainment, flowers, wedding cake and acknowledge gifts as they come in

- advise the best man of anything specific about speech

- choose the grooms wedding ring

- arrange for a rehearsal of ceremony

- if appropriate (it usually is) arrange hen night

The responsibilities of the groom

It is tradition that the groom undertakes responsibility for the legal aspects of the wedding, choosing his best man and the ushers. He will organize the honeymoon, organize clothing for the male members of the family, buy the wedding ring and make a speech. In addition, the groom will obtain the marriage licence. The documentation, ring and church fees are then passed to the best man. The groom should also ensure that luggage is taken to the reception and that a car to take the couple away after the reception is organised.

The role of the father of the bride

The father of the bride will escort his daughter to court and will also escort the brides mother-in-law on going out of the church following the wedding (known as the recessional). At the reception, he will make the first speech. As mentioned, the father of the bride traditionally carries the burden of paying for the wedding. However, this is a matter between families.

The role of the bridesmaid

The chief bridesmaid will be in charge and will look after the younger bridesmaids. She will assist the bride with her preparations on the wedding day. She will hold the bride's bouquet and looks after the brides wedding clothes when she changes.

The role of the best man

The best man will usually be a close friend, either of the groom or the couple together. The best man can be either male or female and will act as an organizer. This will involve ensuring that the ushers are in the right place at the right time and making sure that the groom is dressed and at the church or civil venue on time. The best man will usually be responsible for organising transport.

Once at the wedding venue, the best man will distribute various things such as buttonholes and service sheets and will look after documentation and rings. The best man can also act as witness to the marriage.

When the marriage is over and the reception has begin the best man will introduce the speeches, make a speech himself, respond to the toast to the bridesmaid, read any messages to the couple, look after any gifts received and ensure that the car is ready when the couple depart.

The best man will also organise the stag night and will also dance with the chief bridesmaid as the first dance of the evening.

Role of the ushers

The ushers seat people prior to the ceremony and hand out order of service sheets.

Toastmaster

The toastmaster is becoming more and more a fixture at weddings and will take over some of the duties of the best man. They will formally announce guests to the reception receiving line as they arrive, announce speeches, propose toasts and announce the cutting of the cake.

Paying for the wedding

As pointed out, although it is tradition for the brides father to pay for the wedding, in these more enlightened times families will normally share the burden as much as they can. Traditionally though the following will shoulder expenses:

Groom

- The wedding ring

- Wedding clothes

- Legal and church costs

- Bouquets for the bride and bridesmaids, corsages for the mothers and buttonholes for the best man

- Presents for the best man and ushers

- The present for the bride

- The stag party

- Transport to venue for himself and best man and to the reception for himself and the bride

- The honeymoon

Bride

- The bridesmaids dresses and gifts

- The groom's ring and gift

- The hen party

The father of the bride

- The wedding dress

- Brides mothers outfit for the day

- A wedding present for daughter and future son-in-law

- All announcements, invitations, stationary and photographs and videos

- All flowers for different venues

- Transport to wedding venue for himself or bride, the brides mother and bridesmaid and from wedding venue to the reception for himself and brides mother

- Wedding cake

- Insurance (if any)

- Overnight accommodation for close family if appropriate

Invitations to the wedding

These will differ depending on the type of wedding you are having.

Formal weddings
If the wedding is a formal affair, then you will need to utilise stationary engraved in script, printed on heavy

card. This could include a reply card and envelope. However, there are a number of different types of invitations and the bigger stationers or wedding shops will produce a range of different styles for you to choose from. It is important to be clear on the invitation and indicate whether the guest is being invited to the whole wedding/reception or just to the wedding or to the reception. The examples below indicate the layout of different types of invitation.

1. If the wedding is given by the brides parent's.

Mr and Mrs B Woodward

Request the pleasure of your company

(name of guest)---------------------------------
at the marriage of their daughter

Jane to/with

Edward Woodward

At Halesowen Registry office/Church

On Saturday November 4th 2006 at 2.30pm and the reception after at Summers Hotel Halesowen.

Reply address   RSVP

If the wedding is to be hosted by both sets of parents you should change the wording accordingly. Likewise if the wedding is to be given by the bride and groom.

If the invitation is for a reception only the appropriate form of words should be used.

Preparing the guest list

Traditionally, the bride's mother draws up the guest list in consultation with the bride and the groom's parents. The main thing is to decide on the total numbers of guests for the wedding and draw up the list. Some guests will be invited to the whole occasion and some to only part. If you are having a register office wedding then only the wedding party will attend the reception.

It is important when compiling the list to beware of any special needs of the guests. Maps should be provided with invites showing the location of the wedding venue and reception. When received, tick off acceptances and refusals so that your list is maintained and up to date.

Overleaf is a sample guest list which will help you to compile and monitor the guests for your wedding.

Sample Guest list

Name	Address and telephone	Ceremony or reception	Invitation sent	Gift received	Thank you note sent	Special needs

Alternative invitations

Of course it is up to you how you word an invitation. There is no cast iron rule that you have to follow the laws of convention. The invite should always reflect what you want as much as possible and not what others expect, although with large families this may not always be easy.

As stated, large stationers and wedding shops will have different samples of invitation.

The reception

The receiving line

Weddings differ in the extent to which they follow tradition. At some weddings you will have a formal receiving line. If this is the case, the person co-ordinating the receiving line should be asked to keep the reception room doors closed until after the newly-weds and their parents and the senior attendants are ready to receive guests. This may involve ensuring that a member of hotel staff to guide early guests into a lounge or waiting area and offer them refreshments until such a time as the receiving line is ready. The receiving line is made up of the brides parents, the groom's parents, the newly-weds and their senior attendants in that order, starting with the bride's mother closest to the entrance.

Table seating plan

The top table

The top table will seat the bridal party and there are several plans to cope with different occasions. The most common plan is for nine people with the bride seated in the centre and the groom on her right, bride's mother on his right, then the grooms father and the chief bridesmaid/matron of honour.

This looks as follows:

Chief bridesmaid	Grooms father	Bride's mother	Groom	Bride	Brides father	Grooms mother	Best man	Second bridesm aid

This is the conventional seating plan and sometimes it will not be possible to achieve this. It is up to the bride and groom to decide what they want on their big day. A table should be seated to reflect family but also to take into account situations where problems are likely to arise.

One such situation is where both natural and step-parents are present at a wedding. Alternatives can be discussed with the function co-ordinator when booking a wedding.

Below is an alternative plan for where step-parents and natural parents are in attendance.

Best man	Step-mother-groom	Grooms father	Bride's mother	Groom	Bride	Brides father	Grooms mother	Step-father-groom	Chief bridesmaid

This alternative seats all at the top table but puts a healthy distance between the parties.

Wedding speeches

For many people, weddings are the only time in their lives where they will be asked to give a speech. Wedding speeches are most often given by novices who suffer from nerves and self-doubt. However, this is one of the most important days in the life of newly weds and it is crucial that you make a good speech.

The form

It is usual to have three speeches, and all are toasts. The first toast is proposed by the brides father, or a close family friend or relative. He or she proposes the health of the bride and groom. Next, the groom replies, and proposes a toast to the bridesmaids. Finally, the best man replies on behalf of the bridesmaids.

As with all things, time has changed the usual customs and women are now beginning to assert themselves and make a speech after the groom has finished. Also, best men are also joined by best women.

Each of these speeches need to be prepared in advance and delivered as one would deliver any speech. The following are suggestions for each speech.

The bride and groom

The toast to the bride and groom should express happiness at the occasion and wish them both luck in their new life. It is customary to compliment the bride on her appearance and to compliment the groom on his luck. You may wish to add an anecdote from having known the bride so long, or you may have a funny story about the first time you met the groom. Finish by asking the guests to raise their glasses and drink to the health of the bride and groom.

The things not to do at a wedding speech

- Never make jokes about the bride or mother in law. This is pathetic and outdated

- Never make remarks which are in bad taste

- Avoid smut, innuendo or references to past partners

- Don't use the opportunity to score points

- Keep in mind that this is the bride and grooms special day, so only add to their pleasure.

The Bridesmaids

Next up is the groom, who thanks the proposer of the previous toast and in turn proposes the toast to the bridesmaids. The groom usually compliments the bride on her appearance and thanks her for consenting to marry him. He usually compliments on his good fortune on having found her. He thanks his best man for supporting him, and for working so hard to ensure that the day has run so smoothly. Sometimes, the groom also thanks the bride's family for allowing him the honour of marrying her. However, this is increasingly seen as sexist and outdated. The groom, however, should at least thank the bride's family for accepting him in their home.

The groom then proceeds to tell a few anecdotes before he turns to the subject of the bridesmaids. He should compliment them on how well turned out they are and thank them for attending his wife so well. He will finish by proposing a toast to the bridesmaids.

The main event

The best man's speech is usually the highlight of the wedding. The audience is expected to laugh and the speech is usually timed at between five to ten minutes.

Start by thanking the groom on behalf of the bridesmaids. Add your compliments to both them and the bride.

The usual course of events after this is to say something about your relationship with the groom, and to recount some lively stories about your youth together. If you did not know each other when you were younger then tell a few stories about recent events. While it is expected that you will embarrass the groom slightly, it is important that you do not overstep the mark and ruin his reputation.

Best man's humour

You should not allow your speech to turn into a string of jokes, just for the sake of getting laughs. Never make jokes in bad taste and keep in mind the age and profile of those present. Avoid lewd comments. At the end of your speech, read any telegrams or other communications of good wishes, and introduce any special guests. Keep this section short, as the audience might become restless.

Other speeches

If the bride and groom take a decision to vary this format, they should tell everyone involved and work out who is going to propose which toast.

If the bride wishes to make a speech, she usually takes the opportunity to propose the toast to the people who have made the wedding such a special occasion.

While you are quite at liberty to arrange for as many speeches as you wish, avoid allowing them to go on for too long. It is highly likely that alcohol, food, endless speeches and so on, will all have taken their toll.

Cutting the cake

The last part of the ceremony is cutting the wedding cake. After the speeches the best man (or toastmaster) announces that the cake is to be cut by the bride and groom. The couple will hold the knife over the cake and together make the first symbolic cut. If the cake is large enough, it is tradition for the top tier to be saved for later, for example for the first wedding anniversary or christening.

Display of gifts

It is traditional to display gifts at the bride's parents home. However, a display can be arranged at the reception so that all the guests can view them. Each gift on display should have a name tag attached and should be arranged in order of what they are, i.e. crockery and so on. After the reception, the bride's mother should pack away all the gifts and store then safely until they can be delivered to the newlywed's home.

3

Main decisions prior to a wedding

Setting the date

Theoretically, there is nothing stopping people getting married when they wish. However, there will be constraints relating to the availability of venue and of personnel. For a wedding to be valid in law, the exchange of vows and of rings and signing the marriage register must happen between the hours of 8.am and 6 pm Monday to Saturdays, even if a religious ceremony happens before or after those hours or on a Sunday.

A civil ceremony in a register office can be completed in 15 minutes. A religious ceremony can, however, take place any time anywhere, and last as long as is desired. It can take place in a field, on a mountain-top or anywhere that is chosen.

As a rough guide, a marriage service in a church will usually take between 40 minutes and one hour depending on the minister's address and the length and duration of the hymns. If a communion is included then an extra 20 minutes or so should be added depending on the size of the congregation.

Civil ceremonies and church weddings

If both parties to a wedding are practicing members of a Christian faith, for example, and neither has been married previously, then it is highly likely that a church wedding will be chosen. Even if the couple are not regular church goers, getting married in church may feel right. If this is the case, it is first necessary to find out the name and place of your local church. You will need to call the church and speak to the minister or the priest and make an appointment to see him or her. This will involve both bride and groom.

Depending on when the wedding is planned for, the meeting may be either brief or longer to go into more detail. A further appointment will usually be made to sort out the details, the music, the Banns etc. The date will be entered into the churches diary.

If the bride and groom live in different parishes then both churches and priests/ministers must be visited. The couple will usually be invited to participate in marriage preparation classes and encouraged to join the congregation and attend church if they don't already. A Catholic priest would want to know about a non-Catholic partner's intentions for the future, whether there is going to be a conversion and what faith the children are going to be raised in. A minister/priest is entitled to refuse to marry a couple if they have reason to believe that they are not committed to the ideals of that particular church. The minister/priest will recommend a rehearsal for the ceremony at some stage close to the wedding. All involved with the wedding (with the exception of guests!) should be there for a 'dry run' which will help to calm nerves when it come to the real event.

Civil ceremonies

Many people, for reasons of personal belief and also for reasons of cost, or for reasons such as divorce, choose to marry in a register office. In chapter 1 of this book we discussed the different venues in depth.

In order to be a legal marriage, only the civil part of a ceremony is necessary and the simplest form is that held in a register office. This will be held in the offices of the local Registrar of Births, Marriages and Deaths in a room designated for marriages.

Music can be played during a ceremony, flowers can be brought in and readings can be made. The only element that is strictly forbidden is the religious element.

Most marriage rooms will seat around 50 or so, so it is possible to have a sizeable wedding. Now that more places are licensed for civil ceremonies it is possible to choose larger venues.

Almost all licensed places will offer a wedding package so the whole affair can be conducted at the same place. Obviously, costs will vary with what is required. At licensed venues other than the Register office, a Minister of religion, or one of them, may be prepared to perform a marriage blessing.

Whilst not religious premises themselves, private licensed venues do not carry the same sort of restrictions as register offices.

Marrying outside the United Kingdom

There is an undeniable attraction to leaving it all behind and getting married on some tropical or sun-drenched Isle. Travel agents offer a wide range of packages to many places such as the Caribbean, Mauritius and so on. The travel and accommodation is arranged, as is the paperwork and formalities for the wedding. Travel agents will also advise what documents are needed, both before departure and at the destination. Most of the trips are for about three weeks in length which allows time to obtain any necessary residential qualification necessary to get married.

This kind of holiday with all the trimmings can be expensive. However, if you compare costs to a full blown church wedding, an average being around £16,000 it is usually a lot cheaper. It also compares favourably with a simpler wedding.

Planning the wedding reception

This element of a wedding is usually the biggest single task. It is also without doubt the most expensive part of the day. At one end of the spectrum many couples find themselves having to organise and pay for a meal at a hotel, wine and entertainment. It can become very expensive indeed.

It is possible to plan something smaller and less expensive, such as a cocktail or general drinks reception. After the wedding ceremony guests are invited to join the newly wed couple for drinks, a toast and canapés before they make their getaway.

This kind of function is fine if people's expectations are not that high.

Another way of avoiding all the pressures of a full-blown reception is to hold the wedding ceremony later in the day and invite all the guests to an informal party later, with a light supper thrown in.

Some people, rather than hiring function rooms in a hotel, will put together their own receptions in a local hall or school or similar. For these you will have to arrange a licence for the consumption of alcohol at the local magistrate's court and organise your own entertainment. On the whole, doing-it-yourself is hard work but it is an option and there are mobile catering firms who can assist.

Whichever way you choose to go, it is essential to check the venue out and to get some kind of reference if possible as you will pay the price on the day for a poor venue and poor service. Also, make sure you know what everything costs before you book. As a rough guide to costs for a reception in a three-star restaurant/hotel:

Reception drinks-£3 per head
£30 per head for a three-course meal
£17.50 for a buffet
£12 for a bottle of reasonable wine

If you want to hire an up-market venue such as a stately home this will set you back from £2,000 upwards depending on where and what it is.

A marquee for 50 people can set you back £1500 pounds. Compare and contrast this with doing things on a smaller scale, such as having a drinks party or hiring a community centre and you will have some idea of what the varying costs may be. If money is no real object then make it a day and night to remember. If it is a consideration then scale down the operation. In no way does this detract from the day.

Choosing the menu

The venue should provide a sample menu(s) and wine list. A good hotel should offer choices from finger buffet's to full course dinners with plenty of variety of other dishes such as hot or cold platters and vegetarian dishes. In addition, special diets should be catered for.

Wine and other drinks should be provided with the meal. Also, if the budget includes it you should have champagne on hand for a toast.

Accommodation

Most hotels will offer rooms at special rates to hotel guests and will even, if asked, provide a bridal suite for the newly-weds. If the reception is not at a hotel and overnight accommodation is required then you should book early to avoid disappointment.

Attendants

Anything between one and six bridesmaids (maids of honour) is the norm. The bridesmaids are usually young single females (over the age of six) from the bride's family. If the bride does not have enough relatives then she will first choose from the fiancés family then from close friends. A married attendant is called a matron-of-honour. There is normally only one matron of honour and she will be the senior attendant.

In addition to the bridesmaids other attendants would be a flower girl, pageboy and a ring bearer. Adult attendants are usually assigned to look after the junior attendants.

What to wear
Bridal dress

Shopping for a bridal dress can be time consuming and expensive, depending on what you are looking for. The white bridal gown is the dress most associated with weddings but the range of styles and fabrics on offer nowadays is immense.

A ready to wear dress will set you back from £300 onwards but a designer dress can costs thousands of pounds. Bridal shops will also have an alterations and cleaning service which may be an additional cost over and above the gown.

Hiring a dress

Hiring a dress may be a cost effective solution for the day. Most companies hire a dress out several times and the first hire will be around 50% of the retail value with each time getting cheaper. These dresses are of a simpler design and are washable.

Made-to-measure

If you purchase a dress from a ready-to-wear retailer then it will usually be on a made to measure basis as they don't usually hold stock. The whole process can take up to several months so this is an element that you should plan early, five or six months beforehand if possible. In addition, you will have to have a clear idea of what you want and photographs might help. It is very important that you spend time at this stage as getting the design right is crucial.

Bridesmaids and the Matron-of-Honour

Bridesmaids are usually dressed in a style and colour that compliments the bridal gown. As with the bridal dress, the dresses may be purchased from a ready-to-wear shop, hired for a day or made to measure. To hire a dress costs from around £45 upwards with made to measure and ready-to-wear from around £60. Again, the same timescales apply for purchasing, and the purchase of the bridal gown will determine the style and purchase of the bridesmaids dress.

Dress for the men

As with the bridal dress, what men wear is dictated by the style of wedding. The choice of clothes, at the end of the day, is left to the couple, but it is normal to wear a lounge suit of some description.

Morning suits are popular and most menswear shops will hire them out for the day. To hire a complete outfit of trousers, tail coat, cravat, gloves and hat will cost anything from £100 upwards.

The groom and attendants should, if possible, arrange to hire their suits from the same outfitters who can also advise on style and will be consistent with what they offer.

Transport

Transport is a very important element of a wedding and requires meticulous planning. A car is the most common form of transport hired for a wedding. Cars can be very expensive to hire for a wedding, especially if you are hiring a Rolls Royce or Bentley or stretch limo. Sometimes it is better to make do with your own cars. A look in the vehicle or weddings section of yellow pages will reveal that almost any form of transport is available for weddings, and the prices will reflect the type of vehicle available.

Transport before the ceremony

Transport for the bride is very important, because the bride needs to get to the church on time (as do all others). Whether the marriage is at a church or civil venue there will usually be several weddings going on so it is important that times are kept to.

Before you book the transport, you should at least go and see the company and view the vehicle. You should also confirm how the vehicle will look for the wedding, i.e. how will it be dressed and so on. The things that need to be considered before you make a booking are:

- How often will the vehicle be used on the day, as it could affect your times

- Is there a substitute vehicle in case any problems arise with the chosen one?

- Will the flowers used be fresh?

The vehicle should be arranged well in advance, at least half an hour before the wedding, in order to ensure that it gets to the venue on time.

A second car will be needed for the bridal party. For a church wedding the brides mother and also the attendants will be ferried to church in a separate car. Several trips may be necessary to ensure all are taken to the venue on time.

For a register office wedding, the bride and her father will need transport. The bride's mother traditionally travels alone. However, as with all other elements of a wedding, it is up to the couple to plan accordingly. The most important thing is that all parties travel comfortably, arrive on time and with dignity.

After the wedding ceremony

After the ceremony, the vehicle that transported the bride and other escorts to the ceremony will take them to the reception. It is usual for this car to carry out several trips from ceremony to reception.

After the reception

Most people who get married will leave the reception and go on a honeymoon of sorts. Transport is needed to take the newly weds away to their chosen destination. This can be achieved by using your own car or, if you have had a few too many, then the hire company that supplied the bridal car will also take the couple away. Of course, this will be included in the cost.

Organising photography and videos

Wedding photographers are usually expensive and need to be booked well in advance. You should try to hire one based on recommendation. If this is not possible, then you should ask to see examples of previous work.

The photographer should be willing to take photographs at other venues than the wedding venue such as the bride's house. Obviously, the price will reflect this. The photographer will be at the civil venue before the first guests arrive and will take photos before the ceremony, usually of the main people such as the groom and the best man. The arrival of the bride and her father will be photographed and the walk up the aisle will, if permitted, be photographed.

The usual package of photography for a wedding will include:

• An initial visit to the wedding location to assess the potential for pictures

• A visit to the brides home and reception venue if appropriate

- Up to 100 proof shots from which the final selection will be made

- A photo album

- The chance for others such as relatives or friends to buy copies at an extra cost

- Insurance

The cost for an experienced photographer will be between £500-£600. The more well known, the more expensive.

Video recording of weddings is becoming very popular. The video company will work to a schedule similar to the photographer and they should be booked up well in advance. The costs of a video will, like photography, vary and can cost anything from £300-500 and upwards. Always ask to see previous work.

Arranging flowers

Wedding flowers can be purchased from most florists. They will advise on availability and wedding floral designs are usually chosen from a catalogue or the bride can provide a picture of her own design. Visit the florist well in advance. The most common order is for a bridal bouquet, sprays for the bride's mother and bridesmaids and buttonholes for the groom, the best man, the bride's father and the ushers. There may well be extras for the wedding venue and reception venue and also for the bridal car. The florist can also advise on appropriate flowers if allowed to see a picture of the dress. In this way they can co-ordinate arrangements.

Fresh flowers are usually favourite, although it is possible to get silk or parchment although these generally cost more. The time of year will make a difference to cost. The average expenditure is usually dictated by when the wedding is and what is available. The bridal bouquet is likely to cost upwards of £40, a bridesmaid's spray £30 and buttonholes £4 each. Depending on what you want expect to spend on average £200 on flowers for the day.

The wedding cake

A wedding cake is normally chosen from a local baker who will estimate the size depending on number of guests. The baker will normally have a catalogue and types and sizes can be mixed and matched. The cake itself is usually either a fruit cake or can be a sponge cake. A mixture is preferable. The baker, or the venue manager should be able to supply a cake stand and a cake slice for the day. The overall cost of a cake should be between £100-£150 depending on specification.

The wedding stationary

Like the other suppliers, good stationers will have a catalogue of wedding stationary. Designs are pre-printed with different typefaces to choose from. Details of the wedding are usually sent to the printer several months before the wedding to ensure that there is enough time to cater for mistakes. A matched collection of stationary will include;

- invitations to the church or civil venue only

- invitations to the ceremony and reception

- invitations to the reception only

- reply cards

- orders of service

- table name cards

- cake boxes

- table napkins

- thank you cards

The average cost of stationary should be between £40-60. In addition to standardized stationary it is possible to get personalized stationary from individual designers. Your budget will govern this but on many occasions, couples wish to differentiate the invites and other stationary.

Fees for marriage

These will vary depending on where you get married. As at 2006, the fees for a register office (in England, Wales and Northern Ireland) are:

Notice of intent to marry £30

Payable on wedding day £40

Copy of the Marriage Certificate £7

Church fees are generally not fixed and will vary depending where you are. Larger churches will tend to charge more. A guide is:

The service £175

Organist £ 50

Flowers £ 75-100

Choir £ £75-100

Facilities fee (video) £ 40-70
Bell ringers £50-100

The above is a guide and, as stated, prices will vary around the country. The cost of the Marriage Certificate will usually be included in the cost for the service. If you intend to get married in a church ensure that you get a clear indication of costs beforehand.

Wedding insurance

Wedding insurance is always taken out and any broker will provide you with a quote. A premium will set you back about £75. You may be asking yourselves, what do I need insurance for? It will cover the following:

- Loss or theft or damage to clothing whether purchased or hired

- Loss, damage or failure of photographs

- Illness or death of bride or groom or parent of either

- Failure of supplier to provide goods or services

- Loss or theft or damage to wedding presents
- Loss, theft or damage of wedding rings

Getting your wedding arranged

If you can afford it and cannot bear the thought of arranging your own wedding then you might want to employ a company who will arrange the big day for you. Most companies who do this will act as agents and will leave it to you to conclude arrangements with suppliers.

Wedding gifts

Many couples compile a list of desired gifts, although some prefer to avoid this. The list will almost certainly reflect the needs of bride and groom. Whatever the reason for the list it should be as long and as comprehensive as possible allowing those buying gifts to choose.

There are a number of ways of organising a list, to ensure that the same items are not purchased twice. The bride might choose a shop with branches nationwide and pay a visit to a local branch to see if they can deal with the list. In this way it can be co-ordinated. The list is then circulated to guests who will order, the manager will check the list to see that it has not already been ordered and wrap and supply to the bride. If the item has been chosen a message will be given to the purchaser and another item chosen. An alternative to this is to manage the list yourself. A copy of the list goes out to every invited guest who will call the bride or her mother to discuss their choice.

The bride and groom will usually give a small gift to each of the attendants as a personal thank-you. The gift should be personal to the recipient.

Below is a sample wedding gift list divided into different rooms and items:

Items for the kitchen

- Baking tins
- Bread board
- Bread bin
- Microwave
- Knife rack
- Knife sharpener
- Can-opener
- Carving dish
- Cheese board
- Chopping board
- Fondue set
- Frying pans
- Saucepans
- Kitchen knives
- Mixing bowls
- Scissors
- Spice rack
- Steamer
- Toaster

- Toast rack
- Trays
- Vegetable rack
- Wok

Obviously, you can compile a list of your actual needs from the above depending on what you already have, the same with the lists below.

White goods

- Cooker
- Dishwasher
- Freezer
- Fridge
- Washing machine
- Tumble dryer
- Vacuum cleaner

Electrical equipment

- Alarm
- Blender
- Bread maker
- Coffee maker
- Food mixer
- Hairdryer
- Iron and ironing board
- Juicer

- Kettle
- Pressure cooker
- Radio
- Hi-fi
- Television
- DVD recorder

Cutlery

- Butter knives
- Carving knives
- Fish knives
- Teaspoons
- Assorted cutlery

Crockery

- Cups and mugs
- Butter dish
- Plates
- Coffee pot
- Cream jug
- Cruet set
- Dessert bowls
- Egg cups
- Milk jug
- Sauce boat
- Serving dishes

- Soup bowls
- Soup tureen
- Tea cups and saucers
- Tea pot

Accessories

- Bottle opener
- Carafe
- Coasters
- Corkscrew
- Decanter
- Ice bucket
- Table mats
- Napkin ring
- Wine cooler
- Wine rack

Glassware

- Beer glasses
- Liqueur glasses
- Wine glasses
- Tumblers
- Sherry glasses

Linen

- Bath mat set

- Bath towels
- Bedspreads
- Cushions
- Duvet
- Sheets
- Duvet cover
- Hand towels
- Bath towels
- Napkins
- Pillowcases
- Valance

Furniture

- Bedroom suite
- Cabinet
- Chairs
- Table
- Dining room suite
- Lounge suite

Garden

- Garden tools
- Garden plants
- Barbeque
- Garden shed
- Hedge trimmer
- Hose and reel

- Lawn mower
- Strimmer
- Wheelbarrow

Miscellaneous gifts

- Ashtrays
- Answerphone
- Bath rack
- Bath cabinets
- Scales
- Books
- Candlesticks
- Clocks
- Fax machine
- Linen basket
- Luggage
- Mirrors
- Ornaments
- Rugs
- Pot plants
- Shower curtain
- Sports equipment
- Stepladder
- Telephone
- Tool box
- Towel rail
- Vase

The above lists are not totally exhaustive and the final list will depend on the needs and requirements of the couple.

And finally!

The honeymoon

Traditionally, the honeymoon is taken almost immediately after the wedding, although not always. Arranging the honeymoon is exactly the same as any other trip and, like all other elements of a wedding, can either be arranged for you or you can arrange it yourself. If you are going abroad or plan to go to a popular spot in the UK then arrangements will need to be made early. If you plan to go abroad then you may find, almost certainly will find, that the flights do not dovetail in to your wedding times. This means, as with many couples, that a night in a hotel is required.

Weddings, as well as being fun, can be very stressful as the eyes of many people are on you-you are the centre of attention. For many people, several hours of this can be exhausting. It may well be advisable to book the initial night in a hotel, away from everyone but yourselves and unwind and prepare for the honeymoon proper. Don't forget all the usual if you are planning to go abroad, passports, inoculations etc.

4

Different Types of Wedding Ceremonies

In this chapter we will look at a variety of wedding ceremonies, Anglican, Roman Catholic, Christian Scientist, Church of Scotland, Hindu, Muslim, Jewish, Pagan, Quaker and Unitarian This list is not exhaustive and any register office can advise you on where to get information concerning particular types of ceremony.

In chapter 1 we discussed the requirements of getting married in the UK. In this chapter we will look at various religious ceremonies and how they differ according to the faith.

Anglican Ceremonies

In Anglican faith, the ushers will be the first to arrive at the church. They will know how to seat the guests and have enough orders of service and prayer/hymn books for everyone. In short, their role is that of organising the basics, to ensure that the ceremony gets off to a good start.

Seating is arranged so that in the front pew, on the right hand side sits the groom and best man, with the grooms family seated alongside and immediately behind. The front pew on the left is reserved for the family of the bride and the bride's attendants. The guests will arrive 15 minutes before the service and they will be seated by the ushers-bride's family to the left and groom's to the right.

Close family of both bride and groom are seated at the front with guests seated appropriately from front to back.

After the ushers, the bridesmaids and bride's mother will arrive. After this, the bride will arrive led in by her father. The bridesmaids will assist the bride to make sure that her gown and veil are neatly arranged and secure. They will then take their places behind her, in pairs with the youngest first, and begin to walk up the aisle. As the bride and father enter the church they should give one of the ushers a signal to inform the minister or priest that they are ready. At this signal, the organist will begin to play the chosen music and the groom and best man will leave their seats to stand in front of the chancel steps waiting for the bride and her father.

On arrival at the chancel steps the bride will release her father's arm and the groom will stand on her right hand side with the father just behind the bride. The best man stands on the groom's right. The bride will hand her flowers and any other items to the chief bridesmaid of matron-of-honour so that her hands are free for the ceremony. If there are no attendants she will hand these things to parents or friends.

The minister or priest will begin the ceremony with a short address, reminding the congregation of the solemnity of the occasion and that it is a happy event for the families and for the couple. Guests will be guided by their order of service.

The priest/minister will ask bride and groom separately whether they will take each other as spouse, then will say 'who gives this woman to be married to this man?'. The bride's father will step forward saying 'I do' and will take her right hand in his and place it palm down in the minister's hand.

The minister then places her hand in the groom's right hand and the symbolic gesture of giving away the bride is then complete.

With prior arrangement with the minister or priest this part of the service can be omitted as it is seen as old fashioned and irrelevant. It may also be that the bride has no one to stand with her in her father's role.

The bride and groom now exchange vows and give rings. The best man will place the ring on the minister's prayer book. After the exchange of vows and rings the couple are declared husband and wife and are invited to kiss to seal the ceremony.

At this point, the bride's father will take his seat with the bride's mother in the front pew, likewise the best man will take his seat. The couple will now kneel at the chancel steps to take the blessing and after prayers the minister or priest will lead them to the altar. If there is to be a communion it will be made at this point.

After this ceremony, the newly married couple, their parents, the chief bridesmaid or matron of honour and the best man now go into the vestry with the minister to sign the marriage register. The completed certificate is given to the couple. The organist will then perform for the congregation.

Leaving the church

The procession will form behind the couple as they walk down the aisle. If there is a flower girl she will walk in front of the bride scattering petals as she goes. The pageboy and ring bearer (if any) will follow the bride and groom carrying the train followed by the best man and chief bridesmaid or matron of honour, then ushers paired with bridesmaids. The bride's mother walks with the groom's father and the groom's mother walks with the bride's father as they follow the attendants. As they are walking friends and family will follow in sequence from the front pews onwards.

If it has been agreed, the photographer or video crew can take photos and videos but this is usually not permitted within the church. After the ceremony the photographer will arrange guests for group pictures, with the help of the ushers, and take individual and joint shots of bride and groom. Group shots are then taken.

Blessing services

For those who have been divorced or are marrying for a second time and wish to have an Anglican service to celebrate the wedding in a church where the vicar will not solemnize the wedding, a service of blessing is an alternative option. In such a service, the couple will walk down the aisle together at the beginning, or if she has not been married before, the bride may be escorted to join the groom who is waiting at the altar, while the congregation are singing the first hymn. The couple will then make their promises in front of the congregation as they have already done at the previous civil ceremony.

Buddhist Weddings

Weddings under the Buddhist faith are very rare as there is no prescribed wedding ceremony. It is possible to devise an individual civil ceremony reflecting the couple's cultural traditions and for a Buddhist priest to undertake a blessing.

Catholic Weddings

Any marriages undertaken outside of the Church of England will require a licence. A couple must give notice of their intention to marry to a local superintendent registrar. The marriage itself can be authorised by a priest. If this is not the case then a registrar must be present.

If you want to marry in a Catholic Church you will have to visit the priest and discuss the intended wedding. In relation to the actual ceremony, if the marriage is between a non-Catholic and a Catholic then the mechanics of where you will get married and who attends to give blessing will need to be discussed.

If both parties are Roman Catholic, the wedding ceremony will usually form part of a full nuptial mass. The main elements of the service will cover the significance of marriage, a declaration that there are no lawful reasons why the couple should not marry, promises of faithfulness to each other and the acceptance to bring up children within the Roman Catholic faith.

The service begins with a hymn and a bible reading, followed by a sermon. The priest will then ask if there is any impediment to a marriage and calls on the couple to give their consent 'according to the rite of our holy mother the church' to which each person responds 'I will'. The couple join right hands and call upon the congregation to witness the marriage and then make their vows to cherish one another. Vows are then exchanged, the priest will confirm them in marriage and the best man hands over the ring which is blessed and given or exchanged, with the couple acknowledging them as a token of their love and fidelity. In addition to the ring, the groom gives gold and silver to the bride as a token of his worldly goods. Once the rings are blessed, the groom places the ring first on the thumb of the bride and then on three fingers in turn. Prayers and nuptial blessings follow.

After the final blessing is the dismissal, whereupon the bride, groom and bridal party move into the sacristy to make the civil declaration and to sign and witness the register. If there is to be a nuptial mass the bridesmaids take their seats in the front pew.

For the nuptial mass, the couple return to the sanctuary. They then kneel and the bride is assisted by the groom. If Holy Communion is to be received, those taking it move forward at the appropriate time, returning to their pews afterwards. When the mass comes to an end, the couple proceed down the aisle from the sanctuary, followed by the chief bridesmaid and best man, and then the other bridesmaids, pageboys and parents before the rest of the guests.

Christian Scientist Church

If the minister of the Christian Scientist Church has registered with the appropriate local authority then the Church is licensed for marriage ceremonies. However, as the minister of the church is not usually a registrar then a local registrar will need to be present at a wedding ceremony.

If the church is not registered then the marriage will take place at a local registry but a religious ceremony can take place at the church afterwards.

Hindu Ceremonies

In a Hindu ceremony, the bride will usually wear a red sari with the groom dressed in white. The ceremony is informal and the guests relax even during the ceremony and chat amongst themselves. As with other marriages, if the building in which the wedding is to take place is registered to hold weddings, couples should give notice of their intention to marry so that a registrar can attend the wedding. If a building is not licensed then a civil ceremony will take place beforehand.

At the actual venue of the wedding, the family of the bride will arrange a sacred place, covered with material and with flowers placed in the centre. The bride will arrive first and will be hidden until the groom and the guests arrive. As the groom enters, lights will be waved over his head and grains of rice are thrown to symbolise wealth and fertility. The groom will then take his place with the bride under the canopy and the ceremony will commence.

Humanist weddings

Humanist weddings eschew religion but generally wish for a wedding ceremony that is fulfilling and emotionally satisfying. Humanists have a national network of trained officers. They have produced a book called *Sharing the Future* which contains details of their approach. It also gives details on sample wedding ceremonies. You can choose to have a ceremony which incorporates your own beliefs without the religious element.

If you contact your local Humanist Association you can locate the nearest officiant. See useful addresses at the end of this book. You may if you wish choose a member of your family or friends to conduct the ceremony, which is simple and straightforward. The main focus is on commitment, love and respect for each other, as it is with all other ceremonies.

A humanist ceremony can take the following form:

- Welcome guests
- Readings by the couple, friends and family about marriage, love and commitment

- Vows made by the couple to each other and children

- Exchange of rings or other tokens

- Readings and poems read by couple and family and friends about their future together

Jewish

In UK civil law, a Jewish marriage may be solemnized in any building, at any time of day, provided the couple have obtained the necessary legal documentation from the registrar. Jewish weddings are solemnized either in an Orthodox synagogue under the authority of the Chief Rabbi, or in a progressive synagogue where the civil authority appoints a marriage secretary who is responsible for the legal side of a ceremony.

For a couple to be able to marry under the Jewish faith both must be Jewish. If one is not Jewish they must undertake a conversion prior to marrying. Jewish weddings usually take place on a Sunday, they cannot be solemnised between sunset on Friday to sunset on Saturday (the Jewish Sabbath).

At the wedding the groom and all males must wear hats and the bride a veil. In all Orthodox and most progressive synagogues the bride must keep her hair covered. Prior to the wedding, the couple may be requested to attend pre-marital counselling with the Rabbi.

The Jewish wedding ceremony

The groom will arrive at the synagogue with his father and best man. When the bride arrives, the groom is escorted under a chuppah (silk or velvet canopy, supported by poles). The bride is led into the synagogue on the arms of her father followed by bridesmaids and the mothers of the couple. The wedding ceremony commences with a blessing from the minister. After the ceremony has ended, the couple are left alone in the synagogue room before joining the festivities. At the reception the Rabbi will say grace in Hebrew before and after the meal, which consists of kosher food. At Orthodox wedding receptions, the men dance around in a big circle between courses, holding handkerchiefs so that they do not touch each other. The bride and groom are carried on chairs around the room. There is lots of singing and dancing.

Muslim weddings

A Muslim bride dresses in a heavily decorated gown, and wears a lot of jewellery. Female guests have their head and legs covered. Again, as with all other marriages it will be necessary to ensure that all civil requirements are undertaken. This will involve a prior civil ceremony either in a mosque if it is licensed or at a registry office.

Under Muslim beliefs, a marriage is a contract, and not a sacrament, and thus any lay Muslim male may conduct a ceremony. Women are seated on one side of the Mosque with men on the other. The service commences with a sermon and is followed by a reading from the Koran. The bride and groom give their consent to marry and are pronounced man and wife. There are further sermons and prayers and then the party moves onto the bride's house.

The bride's parents will host a reception, at which guests of the bride bring presents. One week later, the grooms parents host another reception at which the groom's relations and friends bring presents.

Non-conformist weddings

Non-conformist weddings will include Methodist, Baptist, Congregationalist, United-Reform and Assemblies of God faiths.

Their services are similar to those offered by the Church of England but they are more flexible and open to innovation. These churches generally need a registrar official to be present at the marriage, as they are not usually registered to conduct marriages.

Pagan ceremonies

Pagan ceremonies encompass New Age Hand-fasting to formal Druid Ceremonies. Pagans are very much nature based and honour equality and unity with nature.

Hand-fasting is an old Anglo-Saxon word for an agreement between two people. The joining of hands is common in many wedding ceremonies. Many other symbols of marriage may be included in the ceremony, such as sharing bread and wine, jumping over a broomstick into a new life together and exchanging rings and tokens. Weddings are generally held out of doors and attended by a Pagan Priest or Priestess.

Druid marriage ceremonies are attended by a druid or druidess. Guests will form a horseshoe, within which the participants at the ceremony will form a circle. 'Four gates' on the four points of the compass divides the circle. Again it is conducted outdoors.

The ceremony involves the celebrants calling on heaven and earth to witness the marriage, before the couple make their vows. The party walk to the four gates, embracing the elements that it represents-fire, water, earth and air. Vows and tokens (rings) are exchanged and a candle is lit. The couple walk around the circle to be greeted by those present as man and wife, before forming a central circle. Close family and friends make a circle around them and the remaining guests join hands to make a final circle of existence, before a final blessing.

Quaker wedding ceremonies

The Quakers (The Religious Society of Friends) can hold weddings at any time and place. The usual place is the Meeting House normally attended by either or both of the couple. Quaker marriages are a Christian commitment and Quakers, like the Anglican Church, can register their own ceremonies. Like all other marriages, the venue chosen for the ceremony must be licensed, otherwise a civil ceremony will also be required. Marriages where one or both of the couples are divorcees are allowed.

Couples are required to inform their local meeting-house in writing advising of their intention to marry. A meeting is held between the couple and a group of men and women to discuss the forthcoming marriage and its implications.

The service is simple, no procession, music, minister or any other pre-planned element. The couple sit at the front of the Meeting House facing the congregation. The dress is formal but not as elaborate as Anglican wedding ceremonies. Wedding guests can stand and speak at any time. When the bride and groom feel that the time is right to exchange vows they will stand and do so. After they have made their promises, they will return to their seats and the meeting will continue until the elders shake hands to signify that it is over. Rings can be exchanged at any time. Everyone attending the ceremony will go on to the reception.

Single-sex partnerships

The Civil Partnerships Act 2004 sanctioned same sex partnerships giving couples the same rights as heterosexual couples. No religious element is allowed, and the marriage is a civil ceremony conducted in either a registry office or a place licensed to carry out wedding ceremonies. The format of a civil partnerships wedding is exactly the same as that of a heterosexual wedding with slight changes in the wordings of the vows. For more on Civil Partnerships, read A Guide to Civil Partnerships (Emerald Publishing) details at the back of this book.

Unitarian

Most religious denominations view marriage as a holy

sacrament recognised by God. Unitarians view marriage slightly differently as a decision made by two individuals in relation to their own spiritual views and as a freely chosen act rather than a conforming act.

The Unitarian Church welcomes people from different faiths and those who have been previously married. The service itself must contain the legal wording required in all weddings in the UK, the rest of the service is completely individual and may be arranged between you and the officiating minister of that church. You are free to adopt any style that you want. A Unitarian Minister will be able to perform the ceremony at any building registered for solemnization of weddings. The service can be held elsewhere but a civil ceremony must take place first.

5

Planning the wedding-the budget for the day

The planning of a wedding is usually the single most expensive item that a family will have to pay for. It is absolutely essential that you have a well worked out budget for the important day.

As we have discussed, a wedding is like anything else, you will get what you pay for. It is thus very important that you know what you want. A full-blown wedding in a church with a lot of guests can set you back anything up to £20,000. A less elaborate affair will be far cheaper.

Below are several sample budgets which will allow you to see what the potential expenses are.

1. Church of England Wedding

The budget below is assuming 100 guests with all the trimmings, no expense spared:

Budget

Bridal gown and accessories   £1600

Bridesmaids outfits (purchased)	£550
Menswear Hired	£600
Flowers	£500
Photographer	£750
Transport (to church)	£750
Cars	£450
Stationary and postage	£350
Cake	£300
Rings	£300
Reception-including entertainment	£5,000
Going-away outfits	£500
Church fees	£300
Insurance	£95
Honeymoon	£1500
Total	**£13,545**

As discussed, this involves 100 guests and doesn't cut any corners. Obviously, like any form of budgeting, it is best to ensure that estimates and value for money are obtained.

2. Register office wedding

This type of wedding is invariably cheaper, although again it very much depends on what it is you are looking for. A wedding, whether church or registry office, can be as cheap or expensive as you want it.

The below assumes 50 guests with a reception held at a hotel.

Budget

Bridal gown	£500
Outfits	£150
Menswear (hired)	£300
Reception	£2,500
Transport	£250
Rings	£150
Cake	£150
Photographer	£500
Stationary postage	£175
Register office fees	£95
Flowers	£75
Insurance	£50
Honeymoon	£1,500
Total	**£6,395**

This has worked out a good deal cheaper. Of course, with a registry office wedding, you can just pop in with a couple of witnesses and pay the fee and get married and go for a few drinks later. This will cost you almost nothing!

Guide to Planning a Wedding

6

Overall Budgeting for your wedding

It is important, right at the outset, that you put together an itemised budget for your wedding. You should go through each item in turn and obtain quotes and estimates.

- Write them into your budget sheet.

- Remember that an estimate is not a firm quote

- Deal only with reputable companies.

- Once you are happy with a supplier check contracts and confirm all details and bookings.

- Pay deposits on time to confirm bookings

- Allow yourself a margin of 5-10% on costings.

Overleaf is a sample budget breakdown which will be suitable for all kinds of wedding.

COST CENTRE	QUOTE	DEPOSIT
CEREMONY VENUE		
CHURCH/REGISTER OFFICE FEES		
FEE FOR MINISTER/REGISTRAR		
BANNS		
LICENCE OR CERTIFICATE		
BELLS		
CHOIR		
FLOWERS		
MUSIC		
PERSONAL DONATION		
RECEPTION VENUE		
HIRE OF ROOMS		
DECORATIONS		
FURNITURE		
FOOD AND DRINK		
FOOD		
HIRE OF EQUIPMENT		
SERVERS		
DRINKS WITH MEALS		
DRINKS WITH TOASTS		
OTHER DRINKS		
BAR ATTENDANT		
HIRE OF GLASSWARE		
WEDDING CAKE		
ENTERTAINMENT		
MUSICIANS		
BRIDES OUTFITS		
DRESS		
HEADDRESS		
TRAIN		
SHOES		

DEPOSIT PAID	BALANCE	BALANCE PAID

COST CENTRE	QUOTATION	DEPOSIT
UNDERWEAR		
HOSIERY		
JEWELLERY		
GOING AWAY OUTFITS		
BEAUTY TREATMENTS		
HAIRDRESSER		
MAKE-UP ARTIST		
PERFUME		
BRIDESMAID'S/PAGEBOYS OUTFITS		
CHIEF BRIDESMAID'S DRESS HEADDRESS		
BRIDESMAIDS DRESSES/HEADRESS		
SHOES		
HOSIERY		
PAGES BOYS OUTFITS		
MENSWEAR		
GROOMS SUIT		
SHIRT		
SHOES		
USHERS SHIRT/SHOES		
FLOWERS		
BRIDES BOUQUET		
CHIEF BRIDESMAIDS BOUQUET		
BRIDEMAIDS BOUQUET		
BUTTON HOLES		
BRIDES MOTHERS CORSAGE		
GROOMS MOTHERS CORSAGE		
CHURCH FLOWERS		

DEPOSIT PAID	BALANCE	BALANCE DUE

COST CENTRE	QUOTATION	DEPOSIT
RECEPTION FLOWERS		
RINGS		
BRIDES RING		
GROOMS RING		
GIFTS		
PAGE BOYS		
BEST MAN		
BRIDES PARENTS		
GROOMS PARENTS		
USHERS		
PRESS ANNOUNCEMENTS		
BEFORE WEDDING		
AFTER WEDDING		
STATIONARY		
INVITATIONS		
MAPS		
POSTAGE		
MENUS		
ORDER OF SERVICE SHEETS		
PLACE CARDS		
CAKE BOXES		
POSTAGE FOR CAKE		
POSTAGE FOR THANK YOU LETTERS		
KEEPSAKE ALBUM		
GUEST BOOK		
PHOTOGRAPHS		
BRIDE AND GROOM		
BRIDES PARENTS		
GROOMS PARENTS		
COST OF PRINTS		

DEPOSIT PAID	BALANCE	BALANCE PAID

COST CENTRE	QUOTATION	DEPOSIT
VIDEO		
COST OF SERVICE		
COST OF COPIES		
TRANSPORT		
BRIDE AND FATHER TO CEREMONY		
BRIDES MOTHER TO CEREMONY		
BRIDESMAIDS TO CEREMONY		
GROOM AND BEST MAN TO CEREMONY		
BRIDE AND GROOM TO RECEPTION		
PARENTS TO RECEPTION		
BEST MAN		
BRIDE AND GROOM FROM RECEPTION		
DECORATIONS FOR CARS		
HONEYMOON		
FIRST NIGHT ACCOMMODATION		
TRAVEL		
ACCOMMODATION		
INSURANCE		
LUGGAGE		
DOCUMENTS		

DEPOSIT PAID	BALANCE	BALANCE PAID

USEFUL ADDRESSES

Useful addresses

Addresses for copies of documents such as birth certificates etc.

General Register Office for England and Wales
Family Records Office
Smedley Hydro
Trafalgar Road
Birkdale
Southport
Merseyside
PR8 2HH

Tel: 01704 569824

The Registrar general for England and Wales
Office of Population, Census and Surveys
St Catherine's House
10 Kingsway
London WC2B 6JP

Tel: 0207 242 0262

General Register Office for Northern Ireland
Oxford House
49-55 Chichester Street
Belfast BT1 4HL

01232 235211
General Register Office for Scotland
New Register House
Edinburgh
EH1 3YT

Tel: 0131 334 0380

General Register office for the Isle of Man
Finch Road
Douglas
Isle of Man

Tel: 01624 5212

Registrar General for Guernsey
The Greffe
Royal Court House
St Peter Port
Guernsey

Tel: 01481 725277

Addresses for civil and religious ceremony information.

Catholic wedding ceremonies
Catholic Marriage Advisory Council
Clitheroe House
1 Blythe Mews

Blythe Road
London W14 ONW

Celtic ministers

The Pagan Federation
Box 7097
London SW1N 3XX

Foreign and Commonwealth Office

The Nationality Treaty and Claims Department
Clive House
Petty France
London SW1H 9HD

Tel: 0207 238 4567

Humanist ceremonies

British Humanist Association
47 Theobald's Road
London W1X 8SP

Jewish ceremonies

Jewish Marriage Council
23 Ravenshurst Avenue

London NW4 4EE
Union of Liberal and Progressive Synagogues
The Montagu Centre
21 Mapel Street
London W1P 7DS

Office for Overseas Marriage Enquiries

General Register Office
Overseas Section
Smedley Hydro
Trafalgar Road
Southport PR8 2HH

Quaker ceremonies

Quakers (The religious Society of Friends)
Friends House
173-177 Euston Road
London Nw1 2BJ

Scottish Weddings

Church of Scotland
121 George Street
Edinburgh EH2 4YN

Single-sex unions

Lesbian and Gay Christian Movement
Oxford House
Derbyshire Street
London E2 6HG

Unitarian ceremonies

Unitarian Church
Essex Hall
1-6 Essex Street
London WC2R 3HY

Other addresses

Family planning

The British Pregnancy Advisory Service
Austy manor
Wootton Wawen
Solihull
West Midlands B95 6BX

The Brook Advisory Centre
153a East Street
London SE17 2SD 0207 703 7880

Catholic Marriage Care
Clitheroe House
1 Blythe Mews
Blythe Road
London W14 ONW

Tel: 0207 371 1341

The Family Planning Association
2-12 Pentonville Road
London N1 9FP

Tel: 0207 837 5432

Scottish Catholic Marriage care
196 Clyde Street
Glasgow
G1 4JY

Honeymoon
The Association of British Travel Agents
55-57 Newman Street
London W1 4AH
Tel: 0207 393 2000

Information Services

National Wedding Information Service
National House

Freepost 121-123 High Street
Epping
CM16 4BD

Tel: Freephone 0800 009027

Photography

The Association of Photographers
9-10 Domingo Street
London
EC1 0TA

Tel: 0207 608 1441

The Guild of Wedding Photographers
13 Market Street
Altrincham
Cheshire
WAS14 1QS

0161 926 9367

Index

Accommodation 57
After the ceremony 62
After the reception 62
Agreements 30
Alternative invitations 44
Anglican ceremony 77
Attendants 57
Arranging flowers 64

Bridal dress 58
Bride 39
Bridesmaids and Matron-of-Honour 59
Budgeting for the overall wedding 97
Buddhist wedding 81

Catholic wedding 82
Choosing the menu 57
Christian Scientist 84
Church weddings 52
Church of England 19
Church of England wedding 93
Civil ceremonies 23
Cohabitation 28
Cohabitees as husband and wife 29
Common licence 21
Common parenthood 26
Cutting the cake 50

Different types of wedding ceremony   77
Display of gifts   50
Divorced persons and Church of England   22
Dress for the men   60

Effects of marriage   25
Engagement party   33

Fees for marriage   67
Formal weddings   41

Getting engaged to be married   18
Getting your wedding arranged   69
Groom   38
Grounds for annulment   17

Hindu Ceremonies   84
Hiring a dress   58
Humanist weddings   85

Invitations to the wedding   40

Jewish weddings   86
Joint assets   26

Made-to-measure   59
Main decisions prior to a wedding   51
Marriage   15
Marriage and cohabitation   15
Marriage formalities   19
Marriages must be voluntary   16

Marriages which can be annulled	17
Marital confidences	27
Marriages of convenience	27
Marriages abroad	24
Marrying outside the United Kingdom	54
Muslim weddings	88
Non-Conformist weddings	88
Organization of the wedding	34
Organising photography and videos	63
Other denominations	23
Pagan ceremonies	89
Paying for the wedding	38
Planning the wedding reception	55
Planning the wedding -budget for the ceremony	93
Preparing the guest list	42
Publishing Banns	20
Quaker weddings	90
Register Office wedding	94
Religious ceremonies	19
Sample guest list	43
Setting the date	51
Single-sex partnerships	91
Special licence	21
Superintendent registrars certificate	21
Surnames	26

Table seating plan   45
Taxation   29
The Engagement   33
The father of the bride   39
The honeymoon   76
The responsibilities of the groom   36
The role of the father of the bride   36
The role of the bridesmaid   36
The role of the best man   37
The role of the ushers   38
The reception   44
The wedding cake   65
The wedding stationary   66
Toastmaster   38
Transport   61
Transport before the ceremony   61

Unitarian   91

Wedding gifts   69
Wedding insurance   68
Wedding planner   98
Wedding speeches   46
What to wear   58
Witnesses   24

Guide to Planning a Wedding